Casserc

M000084693

& Entrées

Hearty family favorites

quick pasta carbonara

PREP: 20 min. | TOTAL: 20 min. | MAKES: 4 servings, 1¼ cups each.

▶ what you need!

½ lb. fettuccine, uncooked

4 slices OSCAR MAYER Bacon, chopped

4 oz. (½ of 8-oz. pkg.) PHILADELPHIA Cream Cheese, cubed

1 cup frozen peas

¾ cup milk

½ cup KRAFT Grated Parmesan Cheese

½ tsp. garlic powder

▶ make it!

1. **COOK** fettuccine as directed on package. Meanwhile, cook bacon in large skillet until crisp. Remove bacon from skillet with slotted spoon, reserving 2 Tbsp. drippings in skillet. Drain bacon on paper towels.

2. **ADD** remaining ingredients to reserved drippings; cook on low heat until cream cheese is melted and mixture is well blended and heated through.

3. **DRAIN** fettuccine; place in large bowl. Add cream cheese sauce and bacon; mix lightly.

KEEPING IT SAFE:
When a dish contains dairy products, such as the cheeses and milk in this recipe, be sure to serve it immediately and refrigerate any leftovers promptly.

SUBSTITUTE:
Prepare using PHILADELPHIA Neufchâtel Cheese.

spaghetti a la PHILLY

PREP: 25 min. | TOTAL: 25 min. | MAKES: 6 servings.

▸ what you need!

¾ lb. spaghetti, uncooked

1 lb. lean ground beef

1 jar (24 oz.) spaghetti sauce

4 oz. (½ of 8-oz. pkg.) PHILADELPHIA Cream Cheese, cubed

2 Tbsp. KRAFT Grated Parmesan Cheese

▸ make it!

1. **COOK** spaghetti as directed on package.

2. **MEANWHILE,** brown meat in large skillet; drain. Return meat to skillet. Stir in sauce and cream cheese; cook on low heat 3 to 5 min. or until sauce is well blended and heated through, stirring frequently.

3. **DRAIN** spaghetti. Add to sauce; mix lightly. Place on platter; top with Parmesan.

SPECIAL EXTRA:
Cook 1 cup each chopped green peppers and onions with the ground beef.

SUBSTITUTE:
Prepare using ground turkey and PHILADELPHIA Neufchâtel Cheese.

easy shepherd's pie

PREP: 10 min. | TOTAL: 30 min. | MAKES: 6 servings.

▶ what you need!

1 lb. ground beef

2 cups hot mashed potatoes

4 oz. (½ of 8-oz. pkg.) PHILADELPHIA Cream Cheese, cubed

1 cup KRAFT Shredded Cheddar Cheese, divided

2 cloves garlic, minced

4 cups frozen mixed vegetables, thawed

1 cup beef gravy

▶ make it!

HEAT oven to 375°F.

1. **BROWN** meat in large skillet; drain.

2. **MEANWHILE,** mix potatoes, cream cheese, ½ cup Cheddar and garlic until well blended.

3. **ADD** vegetables and gravy to meat; mix well. Spoon into 9-inch square baking dish.

4. **COVER** with potato mixture and remaining Cheddar. Bake 20 min. or until heated through.

HEALTHY LIVING:
Save 70 calories and 9 grams of fat, including 5 grams of saturated fat, per serving by preparing with extra-lean ground beef, PHILADELPHIA Neufchâtel Cheese and KRAFT 2% Milk Shredded Cheddar Cheese.

BARBECUE SHEPHERD'S PIE:
Prepare omitting the garlic and substituting ¾ cup KRAFT Original Barbecue Sauce mixed with ½ tsp. onion powder for the gravy.

CREATIVE LEFTOVERS:
This recipe is a great way to use leftover mashed potatoes.

20-minute skillet salmon

PREP: 10 min. | TOTAL: 20 min. | MAKES: 4 servings.

▸ what you need!

1 Tbsp. oil

4 salmon fillets (1 lb.)

1 cup fat-free milk

½ cup (½ of 8-oz. tub) PHILADELPHIA ⅓ Less Fat than Cream Cheese

½ cup chopped cucumbers

2 Tbsp. chopped fresh dill

▸ make it!

1. **HEAT** oil in large skillet on medium-high heat. Add fish; cook 5 min. on each side or until fish flakes easily with fork. Remove from skillet; cover to keep warm.

2. **ADD** milk and reduced-fat cream cheese to skillet; cook and stir until cream cheese is completely melted and mixture is well blended. Stir in cucumbers and dill.

3. **RETURN** fish to skillet. Cook 2 min. or until heated through. Serve topped with cream cheese sauce.

SERVING SUGGESTION:
Round out the meal with hot cooked rice and steamed vegetables. Or serve salmon on a bed of salad greens.

COOKING KNOW-HOW:
When salmon is done, it will appear opaque and flake easily with fork.

FOOD FACTS:
Check salmon fillets for bones before cooking by running fingers over surface. Small bumps are usually a sign of bones—use tweezers to remove them.

creamy chicken and pasta casserole

PREP: 15 min. | TOTAL: 40 min. | MAKES: 6 servings.

▸ what you need!

¾ cup each: chopped celery, red onions and red peppers

1 pkg. (8 oz.) PHILADELPHIA Cream Cheese, cubed

2 cups milk

¼ tsp. garlic salt

4 cups cooked rotini pasta

3 cups chopped cooked chicken breasts

½ cup KRAFT 100% Grated Parmesan Cheese, divided

▸ make it!

HEAT oven to 350°F.

1. **HEAT** large nonstick skillet sprayed with cooking spray on medium heat. Add vegetables; cook and stir 3 min. or until crisp-tender. Add cream cheese, milk and garlic salt; cook on low heat 3 to 5 min. or until cream cheese is melted, stirring frequently.

2. **ADD** pasta, chicken and ¼ cup Parmesan cheese; spoon into 2½-qt. casserole dish.

3. **BAKE** 20 to 25 min. or until heated through. Sprinkle with remaining Parmesan cheese.

SERVING SUGGESTION:
Serve with a mixed green salad tossed with your favorite KRAFT Dressing.

VARIATION:
Prepare using PHILADELPHIA Neufchâtel Cheese, ⅓ Less Fat than Cream Cheese; skim milk and whole wheat rotini pasta.

easy parmesan-garlic chicken

PREP: 5 min. | TOTAL: 30 min. | MAKES: 6 servings.

▸ what you need!

½ cup KRAFT Grated Parmesan Cheese

1 env. (0.7 oz.) GOOD SEASONS Italian Dressing Mix

½ tsp. garlic powder

6 boneless skinless chicken breast halves (2 lb.)

▸ make it!

HEAT oven to 400°F.

1. **MIX** cheese, dressing mix and garlic powder.

2. **MOISTEN** chicken with water; coat with cheese mixture. Place in shallow baking dish.

3. **BAKE** 20 to 25 min. or until chicken is done (165°F).

SPECIAL EXTRA:
For a golden appearance, after chicken is cooked through set oven to Broil. Place 6 inches from heat. Broil 2 to 4 min. or until chicken is golden brown.

VARIATIONS:
Prepare as directed, choosing one of the following flavor combinations:
Mediterranean Parmesan Chicken: Substitute 1 Tbsp. lemon zest and 1 tsp. dried oregano leaves for the garlic powder.
Parmesan-Onion Chicken: Substitute 2 Tbsp. minced onion flakes for the garlic powder.
Spicy Parmesan Chicken: Substitute ground red pepper (cayenne) for the garlic powder.
Parmesan Pizza Chicken: Substitute 1 tsp. dried basil leaves and ¼ tsp. crushed red pepper for the garlic powder.

KEEPING IT SAFE:
Place frozen chicken under cold running water to thaw. Be sure to use cold water and keep the chicken in its original wrap or place in water-tight resealable plastic bag while thawing it. Also, be careful not to cross-contaminate other food products, work surfaces or utensils with the dripping water.

easy italian pasta bake

PREP: 20 min. | TOTAL: 40 min. | MAKES: 6 servings, 1⅓ cups each.

▶ what you need!

1 lb. extra-lean ground beef

3 cups whole wheat penne pasta, cooked, drained

1 jar (26 oz.) spaghetti sauce

⅓ cup KRAFT Grated Parmesan Cheese, divided

1½ cups KRAFT 2% Milk Shredded Mozzarella Cheese

▶ make it!

HEAT oven to 375°F.

1. **BROWN** meat in large skillet; drain. Add pasta, sauce and ½ the Parmesan; mix well.

2. **SPOON** into 13×9-inch dish; top with remaining cheeses.

3. **BAKE** 20 min. or until heated through.

SUBSTITUTE:
Prepare using regular penne pasta.

VARIATION:
Substitute 2 cups BOCA Ground Crumbles for the ground beef. No need to brown or thaw the crumbles in skillet—simply combine with the pasta, sauce and Parmesan cheese; spoon into baking dish and bake as directed.

SPECIAL EXTRA:
Brown meat with 1 tsp. Italian seasoning and 3 cloves garlic, minced.

turkey-parmesan casserole

PREP: 20 min. | TOTAL: 50 min. | MAKES: 6 servings, 1⅓ cups each.

▶ what you need!

8 oz. spaghetti, broken in half, uncooked

1 can (10¾ oz.) condensed cream of mushroom soup

¾ cup BREAKSTONE'S or KNUDSEN Sour Cream

¼ cup milk

⅓ cup KRAFT Grated Parmesan Cheese

¼ tsp. black pepper

3 cups frozen broccoli florets, thawed

2 cups chopped cooked turkey

▶ make it!

HEAT oven to 350°F.

1. **COOK** spaghetti as directed on package; drain.

2. **MIX** soup, sour cream, milk, Parmesan cheese and pepper in large bowl. Add spaghetti, broccoli and turkey; mix lightly. Spoon into 2-qt. casserole.

3. **BAKE** 25 to 30 minutes or until heated through.

SERVING SUGGESTION:
Serve with a crisp, mixed green salad, a whole wheat roll and fresh fruit for dessert.

taco bake

PREP: 15 min. | TOTAL: 35 min. | MAKES: 6 servings, 1 cup each.

▶ what you need!

1 pkg. (14 oz.) KRAFT Deluxe Macaroni & Cheese Dinner

1 lb. ground beef

1 pkg. (1¼ oz.) TACO BELL® HOME ORIGINALS® Taco Seasoning Mix

¾ cup BREAKSTONE'S or KNUDSEN Sour Cream

1½ cups KRAFT Shredded Cheddar Cheese, divided

1 cup TACO BELL® HOME ORIGINALS® Thick 'N Chunky Salsa

▶ make it!

HEAT oven to 400°F.

1. **PREPARE** Dinner as directed on package. While Macaroni is cooking, cook meat with taco seasoning as directed on package.

2. **STIR** sour cream into prepared Dinner; spoon ½ into 8-inch square baking dish. Top with layers of meat mixture, 1 cup cheese and remaining Dinner mixture; cover with foil.

3. **BAKE** 15 min.; top with salsa and remaining cheese. Bake, uncovered, 5 min. or until cheese is melted.

TACO BELL® and HOME ORIGINALS® are trademarks owned and licensed by Taco Bell Corp.

SIZE-WISE:
Keep an eye on portion size when you enjoy this hearty meal.

SPECIAL EXTRA:
For extra crunch, prepare and bake as directed, topping with ½ cup coarsely crushed tortilla chips along with the salsa and cheese.

20 | Casseroles & Entrées

cheesy tuna noodle casserole

PREP: 10 min. | TOTAL: 49 min. | MAKES: 5 servings, about 1½ cups each.

▶ what you need!

1 pkg. (16 oz.) frozen vegetable blend (broccoli, carrots, cauliflower)

1 pkg. (14 oz.) KRAFT Deluxe Macaroni & Cheese Dinner Made With 2% Milk Cheese

¾ cup fat-free milk

¼ cup KRAFT Light Zesty Italian Dressing

1 can (12 oz.) white tuna in water, drained

1 cup KRAFT 2% Milk Shredded Sharp Cheddar Cheese, divided

▶ make it!

HEAT oven to 375°F.

1. **PLACE** vegetables in colander in sink. Cook Macaroni as directed on package; pour over vegetables to drain macaroni and thaw vegetables. Return to saucepan.

2. **STIR** in Cheese Sauce, milk and dressing. Add tuna and ½ cup Cheddar; mix well. Spoon into 2-qt. casserole; cover.

3. **BAKE** 35 min. or until heated through. Top with remaining Cheddar; bake 3 to 4 min. or until melted.

SUBSTITUTE:
Substitute 1 lb. extra-lean ground beef, cooked and drained, for the tuna.

MAKE AHEAD:
Assemble casserole as directed. Refrigerate up to 24 hours. When ready to serve, bake, covered, at 375°F for 40 to 45 min. or until heated through. Top with remaining cheese; continue as directed.

SUBSTITUTE:
Prepare using 2 (5 oz. each) cans tuna.

layered enchilada bake

PREP: 15 min. | TOTAL: 1 hour. | MAKES: 8 servings.

▶ what you need!

1 lb. lean ground beef

1 large onion, chopped

2 cups TACO BELL® HOME ORIGINALS® Thick 'N Chunky Salsa

1 can (15 oz.) black beans, drained, rinsed

¼ cup KRAFT Zesty Italian Dressing

2 Tbsp. TACO BELL® HOME ORIGINALS® Taco Seasoning Mix

6 flour tortillas (8 inch)

1 cup BREAKSTONE'S or KNUDSEN Sour Cream

1 pkg. (8 oz.) KRAFT Mexican Style Finely Shredded Four Cheese

▶ make it!

HEAT oven to 400°F.

1. **BROWN** meat with onions in large skillet on medium-high heat; drain. Stir in salsa, beans, dressing and seasoning mix.

2. **ARRANGE** 3 tortillas on bottom of 13×9-inch baking dish; cover with layers of half each meat mixture, sour cream and cheese. Repeat layers. Cover with foil.

3. **BAKE** 40 min. or until casserole is heated through and cheese is melted, removing foil after 30 min. Let stand 5 min. before cutting to serve.

TACO BELL® and HOME ORIGINALS® are trademarks owned and licensed by Taco Bell Corp.

VELVEETA cheesy pasta casserole

PREP: 15 min. | TOTAL: 55 min. | MAKES: 8 servings, 1½ cups each.

▶ what you need!

1½ lb. boneless skinless chicken breasts, cut into bite-size pieces

4 cups cooked rotini pasta

1 pkg. (1 lb.) frozen Italian-style vegetable combination, thawed, drained

1 can (10 oz.) RO*TEL Diced Tomatoes & Green Chilies, undrained

¾ lb. (12 oz.) VELVEETA Pasteurized Prepared Cheese Product, cut into ½-inch cubes

▶ make it!

HEAT oven to 400°F.

1. **COMBINE** ingredients in 13×9-inch baking dish; cover.

2. **BAKE** 40 min. Let stand 5 min.; stir until sauce is well blended.

Ro*Tel is a product of ConAgra Foods, Inc.

SHORTCUT:
Have leftover chicken? Prepare recipe as directed, using 5 cups chopped cooked chicken and reducing the baking time to 20 to 25 min. or until VELVEETA is melted and casserole is heated through.

SUBSTITUTE:
For milder flavor, prepare using 14½-oz. can plain diced tomatoes.

three-cheese chicken penne pasta bake

PREP: 20 min. | TOTAL: 43 min. | MAKES: 4 servings.

▶ what you need!

1½ cups multi-grain penne pasta, uncooked

1 pkg. (9 oz.) fresh spinach leaves

1 lb. boneless skinless chicken breasts, cut into bite-size pieces

1 tsp. dried basil leaves

1 jar (14½ oz.) spaghetti sauce

1 can (14½ oz.) diced tomatoes, drained

2 oz. (¼ of 8-oz. pkg.) PHILADELPHIA Neufchâtel Cheese, cubed

1 cup KRAFT 2% Milk Shredded Mozzarella Cheese, divided

2 Tbsp. KRAFT Grated Parmesan Cheese

▶ make it!

HEAT oven to 375°F.

1. **COOK** pasta as directed on package, adding spinach to the boiling water the last minute.

2. **COOK** and stir chicken and basil in large nonstick skillet sprayed with cooking spray on medium-high heat 3 min. Stir in spaghetti sauce and tomatoes; bring to boil. Simmer on low heat 3 min. or until chicken is done. Stir in Neufchâtel.

3. **DRAIN** pasta mixture; return to pan. Stir in chicken mixture and ½ cup mozzarella. Spoon into 2-qt. casserole or 8-inch square baking dish.

4. **BAKE** 20 min.; top with remaining cheeses. Bake 3 min. or until mozzarella is melted.

SERVING SUGGESTION:
Serve with CRYSTAL LIGHT Iced Tea.

bruschetta chicken bake

PREP: 10 min. | TOTAL: 40 min. | MAKES: 6 servings.

▶ what you need!

1 can (14½ oz.) diced tomatoes, undrained

1 pkg. (6 oz.) STOVE TOP Stuffing Mix for Chicken

½ cup water

2 cloves garlic, minced

1½ lb. boneless skinless chicken breasts, cut into bite-size pieces

1 tsp. dried basil leaves

1 cup KRAFT 2% Milk Shredded Mozzarella Cheese

▶ make it!

HEAT oven to 400°F.

1. **MIX** tomatoes, stuffing mix, water and garlic just until stuffing mix is moistened.

2. **LAYER** chicken, basil and cheese in 3-qt. casserole or 13×9-inch baking dish.

3. **TOP** with stuffing. Bake 30 min. or until chicken is done.

MAKE AHEAD:
Prepare and bake as directed; cool. Refrigerate up to 24 hours. To reheat, spoon each serving onto microwaveable plate. Microwave on HIGH 2 to 3 min. or until heated through.

NUTRITION BONUS:
Make this flavorful chicken recipe tonight as part of an easy weeknight dinner. As a bonus, the cheese is a good source of calcium. For complete nutritional information, please visit www.kraftfoods.com.